# May Their Shadows Never Shrink

# May Their Shadows Never Shrink

**Wole Soyinka and the Oxford Professorship of Poetry**

Edited by:
Ivor Agyeman-Duah
Lucy Newlyn

ayebia

An Adinkra symbol
meaning *Ntesie matemasie*
A symbol of knowledge
and wisdom

*May Their Shadows Never Shrink: Wole Soyinka and the Oxford Professorship of Poetry*
Edited by Ivor Agyeman-Duah and Lucy Newlyn



First published in 2016 by the Ayebia Clarke Publishing Limited
7 Syringa Walk
Banbury OX16 1FR
Oxfordshire
UK
www.ayebia.co.uk

**ISBN 978-0-9928436-7-0**

Distributed in North America by Casemate-IPM
www.casemateipm.com

Distributed in the UK and Europe by TURNAROUND Publisher Services at www.turnaround-uk.com



British Library Cataloguing-in-Publication Data
Cover Design by Workhaus, Abingdon-on-Thames, UK
Typeset by Avocet Typeset, Somerton, Somerset, TA11 6RT, UK
Printed and bound by CPI Group (UK) Ltd, Croydon, CR0 4YY
Cover photograph by David Clarke

Available from www.ayebia.co.uk or email info@ayebia.co.uk
Distributed in Africa, Europe, UK by TURNAROUND at www.turnaround-uk.com

Distributed in Southern Africa by Book Promotions a subsidiary of Jonathan Ball Publishers in South Africa. For orders contact: order@jonathanball.co.za

# Table of Contents

# Recommendations for the Book

Wole Soyinka has very importantly shown the world that Africa isn't as it is often represented in the media, a continent riven by civil war, stuck in the depths of poverty and in the clutches of corruption. His rich oeuvre of poetry, plays, essays and memoir powerfully demonstrates that there is complex, finely worked, sensitive art and culture being produced right across Africa and has been for hundreds upon hundreds of years. Soyinka's writing draws from the deep wells of Nigerian and specifically Yoruba myth and understanding, pulling from these sources his core ideas of historical return and recovery, and of creativity as linked to violence and renewal. With the recognition that came with the Nobel Prize for Literature in 1986, and then the nomination as Oxford Professor of Poetry in 2015, the world really sat up and took notice of his astonishing contribution, as the world tends to do when the Nobel prizes are handed out, and it was then that a bright light was at last justly focused on the big resonant themes of his writing and imagination.

**Elleke Boehmer, Professor of World Literature, University of Oxford and Jurist, Booker Prize.**

Art as we know is life and its essence must capture all that is good and not so good about life itself. Professor Wole Soyinka is a spiritual wanderer in the land of the living as well as an expert hunter of the ghosts. That wandering tells us that we are all products of history, whether we are proud of it or not. In this intersubjectivity of being a "product," the artist may be assumed to be offering subjective art and narratives. But that subjectivity can be representational of something fundamental as in the defense of poor people. Intellectual inquiries, even in the paradigm of autobiographical subjective narrative, can frame the objectivity of a place, a person, and in the end of a race. In Soyinka's case, the subjectivity of the permanent state of transition from one chaos to the next becomes the art of liberation, manifested from one text to another.

**Toyin Falola, author of *Counting the Teeth of the Tiger* is the Jacob and Frances Sanger Mossiker Chair in the Humanities and Distinguished University Teaching Professor at the University of Texas, Austin, USA.**

# Foreword

I have thought about Wole Soyinka, about his work and his commitment to justice and to what is right more often than I can say. I have read him, studied him, taught him, admired him, been awed by his intelligence, his eloquence, his humanity and certainly his charm.

Soyinka, famous both as Africa's first Nobel Laureate in literature and an indefatigable political activist is widely and deservedly known as the conscience of Nigeria. As this new book shows, we have many reasons to celebrate this great man.

The facts of Soyinka's life are well known. When he was 33, he was imprisoned without trial for trying to broker a peace with Biafran secessionists and spent two years in solitary confinement in a cell measuring 4-by-8 feet. He has been arrested at least nine times since then, most recently in May 2004, at a rally demanding the resignation of Nigeria's President, Olusegun Obasanjo, whose re-election was widely believed to have involved vote fraud. Soyinka has been in exile three times (I studied with him at Cambridge during one of these periods), and he has had a price on his head no less than five times.

In 1997, Soyinka was tried in absentia for treason and sentenced to death by the military regime of General Sani Abacha. Still, despite great personal risk and sacrifice, Soyinka continues to speak out against injustice, corruption and the lies and brutality of those in power. Whether it was challenging Uganda's Idi Amin in the 1970s, taking to task South Africa's president, Thabo Mbeki, for his years' long denial of the impact of HIV/AIDS on the African continent, or fighting for freedom and democracy in his own beloved Nigeria, Soyinka has been a fearless critic of the abuses of power and those who use their power unwisely and to the detriment of their people.

Although Africa is too often in the West, a geographic shorthand for poverty, disease and tyranny and we too frequently look to it in confusion and despair, Soyinka reminds us that a single voice of conscience can speak loudly and clearly and be a force for change. There is little more hopeful or affirming than that.

Soyinka is Beethoven, inward-looking yet thunderous; he is Armstrong's fierce solo. He is also the twentieth-century inventor of African tragedy. His words have captured our imagination, transformed our thinking, moved us to action and fed our souls. He has made African literature, in all its vastness and beauty, possible.

Playwright, poet, political activist, teacher, student and friend, Soyinka's every aspect is brilliant and he ably deserves to be a model for us all.

I could not think of any candidate more worthy of the Professorship of Poetry at the University of Oxford than this truly great writer, whose works will be read for centuries to come.

*Henry Louis Gates, Jr.*
*Director of The Hutchins Center for African and American Research & The Alphonse Fletcher University Professor, Harvard University.*

# Introduction

In June 2015, an electorate made up of over 250,000 alumni of the University of Oxford was invited to vote for a successor to Sir Geoffrey Hill as Oxford's Professor of Poetry. This post has been open to candidates of all races since its establishment in 1708. But all the successful candidates have been predominantly outstanding British white males.

Among the 2015 nominated contestants was the Nigerian Nobel Laureate in Literature, Wole Soyinka, the second black Nobel Poet Laureate in Literature. The St-Lucian-Trinidadian Derek Walcott, also a Nobel Laureate, had previously been a candidate for the Oxford chair. Both were electoral favourites but ended up not occupying the position. Walcott, 80 at the time, withdrew from the contest after negative media publicity engineered by one of the contesting poets. Soyinka, aware of this precedent, also suffered media controversy and eventually lost to Simon Armitage.

Is the Oxford Professorship of Poetry, which has

been held by such distinguished poets as W.H. Auden, Seamus Heaney and Geoffrey Hill, a provincial accolade? In the following chapters, the contributors attempt to answer this question while also arguing the case for electoral reform without in any way demeaning the victory of the eventual winner.

Chapter One – is a compilation of endorsements from prominent poets, writers and human rights activists around the world who responded to a call for support of Soyinka's candidature. In "Wole Soyinka's Poetry: The Insistence on Liberty," the Romanian poet Carmen Bugan emphasizes the importance of Soyinka's poetics of humanity, his insistence on resilience and liberty. (These endorsements became necessary, soon after the voting had started, because of bad press coverage: they were central to an international grassroots campaign coordinated by Soyinka's supporters at Oxford.)

Chapter Two – "The Election" is by Soyinka's electoral representative, Lucy Newlyn (Professor of English Language and Literature and a Fellow of St. Edmund Hall, Oxford). This gives a detailed account of the 2015 election, calling for reform in the electoral processes. Ivor Agyeman-Duah, author and Development Policy Advisor to The Lumina Foundation (which administers the Wole Soyinka Prize for Literature in Africa) became part of the Soyinka campaign. In Chapter Three, "A Poet of Witness in the World," he evaluates the literary productivity of Soyinka in multi-faceted ways, which include an analysis of the endorsements that make Chapter One. He also explains Soyinka's objective to redeem the stock of Derek Walcott's attempt at enlarging poetry's base, which fell through.

Chapter Four – is a unique Italian insight into Soyinka's work by Tiziana Morosetti. In particular, she reviews Soyinka's book, *Man and Nature* and situates his poetry on an imaginary island in Literary Award and the Canonization of African Creativity.

Chapter Five, the last chapter, is poetry of disappointment, written by those who had fervently hoped that Soyinka would occupy the position.

Ivor Agyeman-Duah
Lucy Newlyn
July 2016

## CHAPTER ONE

# Endorsements
## for the Oxford Professorship of Poetry

Oxford would be fortunate to have Professor Soyinka as its Professor of Poetry. And not because of the "worthy" reasons of diversity and all, but simply because he is one of the best there is today, a poet and thinker who knows both how the world actually works and how the world should work.

**Chimamanda Ngozi Adichie, novelist.**

If Wole Soyinka were to take up the position of Professor of Poetry at Oxford University it would be a great thing for the university and a great thing for this country. Every time he visits our country he is given a great welcome. We love him dearly and to have him share his wisdom and his art at such a prestigious university would be an inspiration to all of us. Ignore the bad mouthing and let's honour one of the world's greatest living writers.

In times like these when we are spending so much time and energy looking inwards and being nationalistic, Wole Soyinka will help us reconnect with the world and be more outward looking. We really need him.

**Benjamin Zephaniah, poet.**

I wish to lend wholeheartedly my support to Wole Soyinka as Oxford Professor of Poetry. His presence would profoundly enrich the poetic and intellectual life of the university. He is one of the greatest literary figures of our age, distinguished and playful, whose grasp of the modern, classical and African world would enable him to bring something very special to his Professorship, his lectures and his interaction with students. It cannot be said too strongly that this is a unique opportunity to bring a genuine legend of contemporary literature into your world. Looking back years later, it would give you cause to congratulate yourselves on a truly inspired choice.

**Ben Okri, poet and novelist.**

It gives me the greatest pleasure to support Wole Soyinka's nomination for Professor of Poetry: he is a massive cultural presence and it would be wonderful if Oxford could provide him with a platform to speak in this way.

**Rowan Williams, poet and former Archbishop of Canterbury.**

Individuals who will stand up for the rule of law against its foes and who will take on the might of an oppressive State, are not only admirable – they are essential. Creating something beautiful to fight the ugliest of human rights abuses and pursuing justice through poetry is truly remarkable. The world is a better place for people like Wole Soyinka and there can be few people who would bring more to the role of Oxford Poetry Professor.

**Clare Algar, Chief Executive of Reprieve.**

Soyinka's poetry – like that of Brecht, Neruda and Darwish – carries its liberating charge in the abundance, wit, craft and lyricism, really in the rhythm and the beauty, of the lines themselves. He is a political poet in that he asserts the value of human life and revolts against the man-made circumstances which reduce it; and he does both those things *by force of poetry*.

**David Constantine, poet and scholar.**

Wole Soyinka would make a unique Oxford Professor of Poetry.

**Tom Paulin, poet and critic.**

I have followed Soyinka's work and writing ever since the Nigerian Civil War. As a former member of the Social Sciences Faculty at Oxford, but also as the foundation Dean of Law and Social Sciences at SOAS, University of London, as an Africanist and as a writer, may I say how much Soyinka means to people I meet on all my travels, including in China, where young people see his work as standing up for the same things they cherish.

**Stephen Chan OBE, PhD, Professor of World Politics, School of Oriental and African Studies, University of London.**

Soyinka's poetry has performed a continual battle against the closures of the mind, wresting us into new forms of awareness and understanding. To encounter the compelling charge of his language, the rare insights of his wisdom and the resonating power of his knowledge, would be an unsurpassable experience for our university.

**Robert J.C. Young, Julius Silver Professor of English and Comparative Literature, New York University (formerly Professor of English and Critical Theory, Oxford University)**

It's wonderful news that Wole Soyinka has agreed to stand for Professor of Poetry. He will bring an African and a world perspective to a post that has tended to be the preserve of (mainly Oxbridge educated) British and American poets and critics. He would remind the insular British that a non-English poet does not simply mean a Scottish, Irish or American one. That would be good for Oxford and for Britain.

**Gabriel Josipovici, novelist and critic.**

The Nobel-Prizewinning Wole Soyinka is more than a fit successor to Geoffrey Hill; to my mind he is the ideal and necessary choice. His poetry, plays and other writings speak from a world and era that are potently still a vital part of our ongoing postcolonial condition. We need to hear his engaged voice and Oxford needs to appoint him, for all that he has to tell us and for its own standing in the world.

**Andrew McNeillie, poet and literary editor.**

Wole Soyinka is a poet and activist of world standing who has faced persecution and suffering with unsurpassed dignity. He is that rare thing: a great writer whose life and eloquence have come together in a valiant struggle for rights and freedom. His election would grace the University of Oxford.

**Ken Macdonald QC, Warden of Wadham College, Oxford.**

Wole Soyinka is a poet of witness in his homeland whose moral, ethical and questioning mindset has guided his poetry and other writing. Such a voice, vigorous, lyrical and purposeful, actively generates hope and would greatly enhance the Oxford Professor of Poetry platform.

**Gerard Smyth, Irish poet, poetry editor of *The Irish Times* and member of Ireland's Academy of Arts and Letters, Aosdana.**

Wole Soyinka's poetry, whether in the earliest verse or in the most recent *Samarkand and Other Markets I Have Known* captures the private instincts while his well-known activism on various fronts reflect the public ones. Yet whatever lyricism we find in his writing is precisely what informs his political sensibilities, for the ethical choices he has made throughout his life have always demonstrated an ultimately aesthetic sensibility. Soyinka is with good reason considered one of the greats of world literature. A son of Africa he may be, but he is both by choice and inclination a gift to the world. He would make an electrifying and very influential Oxford Professor of Poetry.

**Ato Quayson, Professor of English, University of Toronto.**

A wonderful poet and a deserved Nobel Laureate, Wole Soyinka has also been a courageous fighter for human rights over several decades. Pursued and repeatedly imprisoned by dictators who feared him, his shining language of resistance has never dimmed and his sense of justice never faltered. Wole Soyinka's appointment would bring honour to the University of Oxford.

**Shami Chakrabari, Director of Liberty.**

The executive committee of Oxford University Student Union has voted to support Wole Soyinka in the upcoming elections for the position of Professor of Poetry at Oxford University. His poetry and writing has inspired many students, including the executive committee of OUSU. Not only is he an outstanding Nobel-prize winning author, his political activism and bravery are admirable and have been influential to students across the world. We greatly admire his work and encourage alumni to vote for Wole Soyinka.

**OUSU Executive Committee**

Wole Soyinka was one of the most brilliant young writers discovered by the Royal Court Theatre in the 1950s when he was invited to become a member of the original "Writers' Group." In 1958 the Royal Court produced Soyinka's "The Lion and the Jewel." William Gaskill, who directed the play, wrote at that time "I've never met anyone white or black who has that kind of command of language." Nearly 60 years later: the Royal Court is the most important theatre for new writing in the world and Wole Soyinka is one of the great poets of our times. We are proud to support Wole Soyinka as the Oxford Professor of Poetry.

**Elyse Dodgson, International Director, Royal Court Theatre.**

Wole Soyinka is a giant of modern literature – and a man whose life and writing has proved how vitally poetry *matters*. He was imprisoned during the Biafran War, but continued to write, smuggling his poems out for publication. He would be a huge inspiration for the students and staff of Oxford and for poets and poetry across the country.

**Robert Macfarlane, scholar and writer.**

I wholeheartedly endorse Wole Soyinka's candidacy for the chair of Professor of Poetry at Oxford University. I've treasured him as one of the greatest living writers since my college days in the early seventies. Soyinka is not only the most youthful and energetic octogenarian I know, but also a true man of world letters, especially in the English-speaking world. It would be a shame indeed should Oxford University forgo this unique opportunity to be honoured by Wole Soyinka's physical presence and poetic wisdom.

**Rita Dove (Former Poet laureate of the United States).**

Wole Soyinka is quite simply one of the great names of contemporary literature. Oxford would be mad not to endorse his nomination as its Professor of Poetry. In my long experience of his work and of the man himself I have absolutely no doubt that he would be conscientious in the role, illuminating in his lectures and link the university in unexpectedly exciting ways with many corners of the world. When I ran the Africa Centre in London he supported our work and in subsequent years when I was Director of Literature at Arts Council England and then at the British Council I always found Soyinka added vitality and intellectual stamina to any event in which he agreed to participate. I hope Oxford will not look a gift horse in the mouth.

**Alastair Niven, formerly Director-General of the Africa Centre in London, Director of Literature at the Arts Council and Director of Literature at the British Council.**

I am delighted that Wole Soyinka has allowed his name to be put forward for this post and that he has not issued some "statement" about poetry to flatter the hearts of some presumed electorate. The choice, as he knows, is literary, not political and like his own tiger, he does not "shout his tigritude" but acts. He will be a wonderful professor. The suggestion made recently by a television presenter that his age is against him is exactly wrong.

**Michael Schmidt, poet, author, scholar and publisher.**

More than fifty years ago, Wole Soyinka, in his poem "Telephone Conversation," portrayed with ferocious humour the dark ironies of a black man trying to rent a room from a white landlady. Hopefully now, in a better time, Oxford will welcome and learn from him.

**Amit Chaudhuri (Professor of English and Novelist).**

Wole Soyinka will bring a whole continent to Oxford and will inspire poets and the public alike with his urgent concerns for humanity as well as the highest artistic achievement. I think he is absolutely indispensable here.

**Carmen Bugan, Poet.**

As a poet, playwright, director, actor, novelist and essayist, Soyinka has been eloquent and passionate in denouncing the injustices of both foreign and internal colonialism in Africa. His courage has repeatedly landed him in jail, with periods of solitary confinement. He has remained stubbornly, even heroically faithful not only to his vision of social justice but also to his often difficult, compressed, uncompromising art. A dazzling poet who is also a thunderous lecturer who has lived an extraordinary life of struggle, he will bring to the Professorship an exceptionally strong combination of gifts, skills and knowledge.

**Jahan Ramazani, University Professor and Edgar F. Shannon Professor of English, University of Virginia.**

Wole Soyinka is that rare thing; a master both of words and action. A concerned humanist in his politics and a committed activist in his writing and vice versa. His writing alone more than qualifies him for the post, in addition to which he is the most wonderful speaker and original thinker. I can't imagine a more fitting or overdue appointment. How very fortunate Oxford would be to have him.

**Tamsin Oglesby, playwright.**

Soyinka's corpus calls to mind the root of the word "poet" in the Greek *poiein,* "to make" or, as he puts it in the prefatory note to his early poem "Idanre", the capacity of poetry to "erase known worlds," boldly breaking apart to create the new. In his poems, mythology and modernity, tradition and experiment, ethereality and earthliness collide. Soyinka's technical skill and range, intellectual bravery and commitment to justice are unmatched by any poet of his generation. It would be a real privilege for the University of Oxford to have him as the next Professor of Poetry."

**Natalya Din-Kariuki, Rhodes Scholar, University of Oxford.**

When Yale University conferred an honorary Doctor of Letters degree on Wole Soyinka in 1980, I was asked to write the formal citation, which reads as follows: "Poet and playwright, in a language metaphorical and lyrical, you have redefined modern tragedy through a synthesis of Yoruba and Western tragic forms. In the face of certain persecution, you boldly accepted the role of spokesman against tyranny in all its pernicious forms. Yours is a constant cry against racism and fascism and for justice and equality without regard for your personal safety. Undaunted force for freedom, master of the verbal arts, we at Yale salute you with the degree of Doctor of Letters." To those words, I would only add that Soyinka is one of the very few people in the world who could have just as easily been awarded the Nobel Prize for Peace as the Nobel Prize for Literature. And through his remarkably rich and ample corpus of books of poetry and drama, created over more than five decades, he has consistently pushed the limits of the English language to register an African metaphysical world-view. As Penelope Gilliatt wrote in 1965 of his great play, "The Road," "Every decade or so, it seems to fall to a non-English dramatist to belt new energy into the English tongue… Wole Soyinka has done for our napping language what brigand dramatists from Ireland have done for centuries: booted it awake, rifled its pockets and scattered the loot into the middle of next week." I can think of no better way to describe Soyinka's magnificent poetic diction and I can think of no candidate more worthy of the Professorship of Poetry at the University of Oxford than this truly great writer, whose works will be read for centuries to come.

**Henry Louis Gates, Jr, The Alphonse Fletcher University Professor, Harvard University.**

# Wole Soyinka's Poetry
## The Insistence on Liberty

*Carmen Bugan*

*As voting for Oxford University's next Professor of Poetry gets underway, Dr Carmen Bugan writes a special dispatch on the poetics of – and humanity in – the work of Nigerian Nobel Laureate Wole Soyinka, who is one of five nominees in the running for the position.*

The Nobel Laureate Nigerian writer Wole Soyinka has recently been nominated to the post of Professor of Poetry at Oxford and voting is currently taking place. This welcome and ground-breaking nomination – if elected, Soyinka will be the first ever African to hold the post – brings a renewed attention to his poetry, which is part of an extraordinary opus including drama, novels, memoirs and criticism. Soyinka writes in English and he brings to the language rich flavours of African names, folklore and landscape, in a register that marries his country's heritage with European tradition. Like his other writing, his urgent poems draw deeply from the mythology of the Yoruba tribe and the local culture, yet they reverberate with what he calls his "abiding religion – human liberty."

Soyinka's poetry crosses the Mediterranean like a boat loaded with African people risking their lives, whether in search of freedom or simply a better life. His poem "Migrations" has recently been etched on the graves of refugees who did not reach the shore of Italy breathing. Soyinka's poem, called by the Italian authorities a *carezza* (a caress, soothing touch) gives dignity to those who died and comfort to their families. It bridges the deadly gap between a continent that sheds its people into the sea and a continent that looks bewildered at the human loss. It rests at the uncomfortable boundaries between those who have and those who have not, remaining engaged with the real world.

Born in 1934 and educated in Nigeria, Soyinka took a doctorate from the University of Leeds in 1973 and worked at the Royal Court Theatre in London. In 1960 he returned to Africa. His writing opposes colonialism and political corruption, and reflects a commitment to the dignity of people. In 1967, during the Civil War in Nigeria, Soyinka wrote an article in which he appealed for ceasefire. For this he was imprisoned and sent into solitary confinement for nearly two years. His experience as prisoner led to work imbued with a personal sense of sacrifice – a personal testimony – for the way in which poetry fights for justice. His collection of poems *A Shuttle in the Crypt*, which he describes as "a map of the course trodden by the mind, not a record of the actual struggle against a vegetable existence," intimates to the reader the agonies of solitary confinement. His poems are by turn meditative, prophetic and angry. Yet they breathe a sense of resilience. In the poem "To the Madmen over the Wall", he refuses descent into madness even as he shows to the reader the extent to which the mind is wrung by incarceration:

*Howl, howl*
*Your fill and overripeness of the heart,*
*I may not come with you*
*Companions of the broken buoy*
*I may not seek*
*The harbour of your drifting shore.*

'When Seasons Change' meditates on the solitude of confinement in high register:

*Shrouds of seasons gone, peeled*
*From time's corpses, mouse-eaten thoughts*
*You flutter upon solitude in winds*
*Armed in shrapnels from the shell of vision*
*Veils on the altar of unplighted troths*
*Cobweb hangings on the throne of death*
*In solitude.*

Wilfred Owen's war poems, W.B. Yeats, Eliot and Shakespeare come to mind when reading these lines. In a world where engaged poetry either sounds like propaganda or is ignored as such, there is a lot to learn from Soyinka's defiant language and his ability to face the hard truths as a poet.

Since 1986, when Wole Soyinka received the Nobel Prize for Literature for works in which he "fashions the drama of existence" with "poetic overtones," he has been sought as a speaker and lecturer all over the world whilst continuing to hold teaching posts in Nigeria. He brings with him the feeling of the wider human community and a sense of conviction about art's necessity when dealing with difficult subjects.

When I first came to Soyinka's work in the late 1990s, it was these lines that kept going through my mind: "Slaves do not possess their kind. Nor do / The truly free" ("Funeral Sermon, Soweto," from *Mandela's Earth and Other Poems*). Soyinka writes about the discomfiting reality of our "civilised world" with devastating clarity and depth. He shows the gap between the free-kind and the slave-kind of the human race, pointing to a solution. What makes me return to Soyinka's poems is his insistence on resilience and liberty and the way in which he works this insistence into a language that remains in the heart and mind long after the book is closed.

**CHAPTER TWO**

# The Election

*Lucy Newlyn*

The election of an Oxford Professor of Poetry is always of interest to the British Press for obvious reasons. With an electorate of more than 250,000 Oxonians scattered all over the world, this is a unique post which attracts candidates of the highest international standing. Even the bookies take an interest in predicting the results.

But should the appointment of a Chair at Oxford be subject to the amount of pressure that is routinely involved in the intense media attention? Is it time that the system changed?

This year – 2015, for the second time in six years, a candidate of absolutely outstanding distinction has been subjected to disparaging remarks in the press during the electoral process. The remarks made about Wole Soyinka (Nobel Laureate, 1986) in *The Sunday Times* were regrettable in every way; and though he responded to them with characteristic wit and dignity, they unquestionably caused personal hurt.

It is of course possible to overestimate the damage done to Professor Soyinka's candidacy by this article. One hopes that most *Sunday Times* readers immediately typed his name into Google – where they will have found a reassuring treasure-trove of interviews, lectures, poems, news-footage and other evidence of his abundant energy and current creativity. One trusts that the overwhelming supply of online material will have enabled them to form their own views about his readiness and ability to perform the various duties of this post.

What is certain is that an unpleasant whiff of "negative campaigning" was introduced into what had hitherto been an entirely unruffled electoral process. I had to react quickly as Soyinka's representative to redeem his candidature – not just by making a statement in *The Guardian*, but by enlisting help in rounding up a collection of endorsements from writers all over the world, distributing publicity flyers and setting up a Facebook page. Up till the intervention of *The Sunday Times*, no one had been thinking in terms of having to justify nomination of one of the world's greatest poets; but thereafter the support for Soyinka turned into a grass-roots campaign.

Given Soyinka's stature, not just as a writer but as a much-loved and greatly respected champion for human rights, it is understandable that many people across the world are left puzzled, disappointed and angry with the result of the 2015 election. It is a depressing thought that the outcome may have been influenced by press intervention. Negative campaigning – distasteful under all circumstances – is especially regrettable in this case because it lays the University open to charges of parochialism.

If elected, Wole Soyinka would have been the first African Professor of Poetry at Oxford, as well as the first black African appointee in the English Faculty: a historical appointment of immense symbolic importance. Of course the university has no control over the outcome of the election – it is a democratic process involving (potentially) hundreds of thousands of alumni; but this is not always understood or remembered outside Oxford. At the point when the results are announced it is always "Oxford" (the institution) that carries the responsibility for the outcome.

The press has a vested interest in stirring up unnecessary controversy and their attention is to trivia more than to substance. Although doubtless incorrigible – mischief is, after all, more entertaining to readers than conscientiousness –there ought to be some way of balancing or counteracting the deleterious effect they can have on the public image of a candidate. The honour of distinguished writers is at stake, as is the university's own international reputation. Unless Oxford University takes steps to prevent this happening again, we will find that in future the most outstanding candidates in the world – people of the calibre of Derek Walcott and Wole Soyinka – will be unwilling to accept nomination. It is especially important that the university takes a stand on this, because of issues concerning diversity and internationalism. Why not send out a stronger signal that "Professor of Poetry" does not necessarily mean "English Professor of Poetry" or "Professor of English Poetry"? Oxford should not allow its international standing to be compromised by the parochial agendas of the British press. We have – among many other resources – a superb reputation in postcolonial studies, a distinguished Centre for African Studies, a Humanities division in which academics are producing world-class research on literature in many languages. It is sad indeed that the hard work these people are engaged in is (implicitly) undermined by the press, who inevitably show favouritism towards "home-grown" talents.

One obvious method for reducing press influence would be to turn this Chair into a regular post, analogous to other senior appointments in the university – with a search committee, references and a confidential selection process. If we went down this route, it would be inappropriate for the committee to consist solely of Oxford academics. We should be looking for candidates of the very highest quality, who will stretch our students to the full. To ensure that we look as far afield as possible, in a spirit of adventurousness and diversity, we would need to have some strong input from outsiders. Nominations should be called for from Convocation. The selection committee considering these would need to include outstanding writers from around the world.

After the experience of acting as Wole Soyinka's representative, I confess that I am drawn to the idea of a confidential committee, for one reason and one reason only: that it would considerably reduce the influence of the press. In all other respects, I am in favour of keeping this post as the unique and wonderful oddity that it is – the only elected position of its kind in the world, involving a huge electorate and giving poetry a very high profile.

Assuming that the post continues as an elected one, it would be in the University's best interest to ensure that personal representatives of candidates are given access to a press official, who will advise them and enable documents to be released in response to inaccuracies or misleading information in the press. Regularisation of the way in which this is done would be the University's responsibility, and could be managed fairly and equitably.

There are additional ways in which the election can and should be improved in future years. For such a high profile post, the 2015 election was given remarkably little advance publicity by the university press office. Many voters complained about inaccessibility of information concerning the nominations and electoral process – a major factor in the poor voting turnout. There were also difficulties with online registration, a cumbersome two-stage process. Unless problems such as these are addressed, the university is in danger of excluding a large part of its international electorate. If most of the voters are from the UK, then the probability of a parochial outcome is increased.

And talking of inclusivity, isn't it time for students to be given the vote? The electorate for this professorship consists of more than 250,000 people. In 2015, of those voting, 25% were members of Congregation and based in Oxford; the remainder were alumni. The majority of people who voted in the election will never attend a single lecture given by the Professor of Poetry they have elected. Meanwhile, the student population of this university – the very people who will be here during term-time, ready and able and willing to attend the lectures – is disenfranchised. Unrest about the unfairness of the current system is growing among the junior members and after this year's election many of them are particularly vocal because the candidate they preferred has failed to win. (The executive committee of OUSU gave Soyinka a ringing endorsement.) I propose that next time round the election for this post is opened to all matriculated members of the university.

I have submitted a report on the election, outlining

a number of possible reforms and look forward to the resulting discussion as it passes through university committees. Meanwhile – on a happier note and putting aside all criticisms of the system – we must be grateful that such a good poet has won the election. Congratulations to Simon Armitage and I wish him the very best for his tenure of the professorship.

## CHAPTER THREE

# A Poet of Witness in the World

*Ivor Agyeman-Duah*

It was anticipated to be a mere formality as night fell on the ballot on 19th June 2015, that the Nobel Laureate, Wole Soyinka would be confirmed as the Oxford Professor of Poetry.

I had been part of the campaign by kind invitation from Lucy Newlyn, Soyinka's electoral representative at Oxford. Almost a year to this election, Soyinka had given an extra-ordinary lecture: "*Literature, the African Condition and My Life*" at the Sheldonian Theatre at the University. He had been introduced by the Vice-Chancellor, Andrew Hamilton on the occasion of the 2014 African Studies Centre Annual Lecture at Oxford. Soyinka was on his feet for an hour-and-a-half on that bank holiday (Monday 5 May), defying his newly acquired octogenarian status. The anthology, *Essays in Honour of Wole Soyinka at 80* (Ayebia Clarke: 2014) which comprised one of the most diverse collections of essays published on his personality and work, with contributions from fellow Noble Laureates and some African leaders was also launched at the venue.

That bank holiday event and its large audience had everything to do with Soyinka's presence and his human rights activism.

My mind went back to 50 years ago. Soyinka had re-gained his freedom from prison after the Biafran Civil War and been given a two-year fellowship at Churchill College, Cambridge. His series of lectures there would be published later as, *Myth, Literature and the African World.* However, the faculty did not regard African literature "as a serious area of study within the "English Tripos" and led him to accept an appointment in Social Anthropology. But that was in the mid 1970s and the beginning of the de-colonization of the academy. He had at that time not published, *Ake: The Years of Childhood* (1981) a classic memoir in English literature and it would be at Cambridge that his famous play, *Death and the King's Horseman* would be written.

By this time in Europe as in Africa, Soyinka had made strong inroads. The Royal Court Theatre in London, always keen to promote his talents had produced his play, *The Lion and the Jewel* in the 1950s as a member of the Writers Group. As the current leadership of that institution says through Elyse Dodgson, the International Director on behalf of their predecessor, William Gaskill, who directed the play: “I’ve never met anyone white or black who has that kind of command of language.”

Ngugi wa Thiong’o, the distinguished East African writer and academic, recalls Soyinka’s Royal Court Theatre days as an inspiration to Africans like him who were in search of role models.

When the result was announced, Soyinka was in Los Angeles (where he lives) and was preparing to undertake one of his relentless travels: to New York transiting through London to Accra where he was to be the guest of honour at the 60th anniversary celebrations of the Ghana International School (GIS) in Accra. He took the announcement in his stride with such wit and candor that disarmed any cause for unease.

He wrote:

*A Huge personal thanks to you, Ivor. I’ve just sent this message to Lucy for the Campaign team.*

*“The votes have been cast and the new Oxford Professor of Poetry elected. I raise a huge goblet to my main sponsor, Professor Lucy Newlyn – upon whom I have bestowed the title of Eleto Ab’ija N’badi – Strategic Grand Marshal – and to her creative team of campaigners and supporters, her family and all. They all share the responsibility for getting me truly caught up in the excitement generated by this historic union of*

*the poetic and democratic Muses. As we say at home, may their shadows never shrink.*

*(Mind you, if only they'd allowed me to import a small team of our seasoned electoral jugglers from the home front…. ah well!)*

*I must now concede a secret regret! What I had wistfully nursed as my "Derek Walcott" agenda must sadly be relinquished. In my view, one of the three most invigorating poets of this age, acceptance of my own nomination – as I frankly admitted to my sponsors – was significantly propelled by the thought of "serving out his time," Derek's 2011 candidature, as we all recall, having been thwarted by some lamentably unpoetic conduct in that campaign. All that however, are in the chronicles of the past.*

*Finally, to Simon Armitage, a strong hand of fellowship and may his fount of inspiration never run dry."*

*Once again, to All, All and All, my sincerest thanks.*

*Wole SOYINKA.*

When I met him at the Accra international airport, he was himself again. And then three days later, he would continue his round of global lectures in Germany, Italy, Lagos and Accra, finally returning to Los Angeles.

Soyinka's robust travel routine and work on intercontinental flights is part of his spirit and fulfilment of promises made. When a UK member of the House of Lords expressed the view that Soyinka was too grand (and too old!) and would not bother to come to Oxford to fulfil the obligations of the post should he be voted for, that person exhibited a measure of misunderstanding which is difficult to justify. An inestimable opportunity in the history of Oxford University was therefore lost.

There seems a sense in which a degree of nationalism played a part in the final election of the winner, Simon Armitage however worthy. The reasons for the need for electoral reform as indicated by Lucy Newlyn and others are obvious if Oxford, post-empire is to avoid a reputation for academic insularity and non-acceptance of those not like themselves.

When a case was made for the internationalization of the Booker Prize, there was fierce resistance from the literary elite in England and their confidence in English and British writers controlling it from within the Commonwealth as paramount.

The philosopher, Kwame Anthony Appiah's riposte to Chinua Achebe not winning the Booker Prize was: "… In things like the Booker Prize, if they pick somebody who is not English, they want someone who is sort of a little bit exotic. Achebe is an elegant English prose stylist, but he is not stylistically exotic – that is, he writes the way Thomas Hardy wrote…" Now that must be even more confusing for England's expectations.

If you put literature aside, in a further inquisition into attitudes of Englishness and empire-building and the economic domination of the past, one can appreciate the current concern over the rising economies of East Asia and the threat to England's declining world influence. But a strategy of inward looking does not help a feeling of decline. Bearing this in mind then, the retention of the Oxford Professor of Poetry within is understandable and does not demean Armitage's own poetic prowess.

This re-engineering of foreign policy done with the knowledge that a few years ago, criticism against China (sometimes for no apparent reason) was part of the daily staple of the media. The Prime Minister, David Cameron was the first to warn Africa and other developing nations to be wary of Chinese neo-colonial activities in Africa yet, Cameron himself travelled with the largest trade delegations to China to negotiate hundreds of millions of pounds worth of business deals for British companies.

Chimamanda Ngozi Adichie has had difficulty relating to her African literary elders especially in public discussions or commentary on them. The first time I read her views on such a stance (apart from the funny encounter with Chinua Achebe) was when she paid a glowing tribute to the Ghanaian playwright and poet, Ama Ata Aidoo for influencing her writing.

Let us examine her endorsement of Soyinka: "Oxford

would be fortunate to have Professor Soyinka as its professor of poetry. And not because of the "worthy" reasons of diversity and all, but simply because he is one of the best there is today, a poet and thinker who knows both how the world actually works and how the world should work."

Soyinka's intercontinental flight itinerary means that for four out of 12 months of the year, airlines are his natural habitat and the cabin crew his family. The issues he travels around the world to discuss and protest against are the way he sees how the world should work on a more humanist level.

In September 2014, he flew from Los Angeles to Nairobi, Kenya's capital to be a guest speaker at the Storymoja Literary Festival. This proved a difficult trip because the connecting flights were cumbersome but he wanted to honour his friend, the late Ghanaian poet, Kofi Awoonor who had been killed the previous year (as a guest speaker) when terrorists attacked the Westgate Mall in Nairobi. Awoonor had gone to have breakfast with his Nairobi-based son and was caught up in the crossfire. Because of the flight difficulties, Soyinka arrived at dawn on the day and had only six hours rest before his speech.

What he did, since the platform was also for The Wangari Maathai's Memorial Lecture was to combine an environmental management and reforestation issue with literature titled: *Parables From Wangari Maathail's*

*Tree.* Wangari had become the first African woman to win the Nobel Peace Prize in 2004 after a huge revolution in Kenya of tree planting and sustainable development through her Green Belt Movement. This was long before climate change became a science

Soyinka's life has been like that: combining the poetic with public policy. He spoke against the slaughter of Igbos in the Biafran Civil War (his refrain to the federal forces to "think again") at great risk to his personal safety. He also took a stance against and demanded justice for the "comfort women" of Korea who were at the mercy of Japanese soldiers with imperial goals in the Far East. He was the first poet of international prominence to call for the defiance of both the Organization of African Unity (now the African Union) and the United Nations notions of territorial integrity and "invade" Rwanda to save thousands of lives from the genocide in 1994.

Soyinka, prior to winning the Nobel Prize had not only used his influence to bring to greater attention scattered poetry of the newly independent Africa in anthologies such as, *Poems of Black Africa* but used the Nobel address titled "This Past Must Address Its Present" to chronicle world issues on injustice and racism. He wrote on dictatorship as much as on environmental issues in such works as, *A Play of Giants* and *Kongi's Harvest*, to oil spillage in the Niger Delta, Nigeria in *Swamp Dwellers* to inhuman conditions in

Guatemala and elsewhere. Ridding South Africa of apartheid became his personal crusade.

Some have accused him of being a lone ranger who undertakes projects which might need multiple levels of support and co-operation. But apart from the editorship of *Poems of Black Africa,* he also brought under his influence diverse voices and talents in his compilation and CD readings in *A Poet's Guide to Mandelaland*, an anthology of poetry as a tribute to Mandela's passing. Apparently, he knew that multiple voices would make a greater impact.

As Secretary-General of the Union of African Writers, he led a crusade to dislodge dictators in East and Central Africa including Idi Amin and Emperor Bokassa in the 1980s. As President of the International Parliament of Writers, he met leaders of South Korea (and other East Asian countries) to discuss human rights issues.

When Chimanmanda Ngozi Adichie, like Clare Algar, the Chief Executive of Reprieve endorsed his bid for the Oxford Professor of Poetry position (Algar did so with institutional approval), they expressed the hope that Soyinka would bring such universal largesse and presence to Oxford as was evident in Algar's endorsement:

"Individuals who will stand up for the rule of law against all odds and who will take on the might of an oppressive state are not only admirable, they are essential. Creating something beautiful to fight the ugliest of human rights abuses and pursuing justice through poetry is truly remarkable. The world is a better place for people like Wole Soyinka…"

Before Soyinka arrived in Accra for the GIS programme, a CCTV crew at their Nairobi bureau in Kenya flew to Accra to make a documentary on him for Chinese television. The producer, a Dutchman, had virtually read everything Soyinka had written because his audience in China are very keen to hear whatever Soyinka has to say. The Chinese Academy of Arts and Sciences have invited Soyinka to China recently on a few occasions and he has a considerable following there.

As Stephen Chan at SOAS (with a Chinese ancestry) puts it: …"As an Africanist and writer, may I say how much Soyinka means to people I meet on all my travels, including in China, where young people see his work as standing up for the same things they cherish."

If Soyinka were to be regarded just as a Yoruba specialist, it would be difficult to imagine how he could bond with the Chinese youth of today.

The interview with the Chinese crew gathered momentum on art, mediation and spirituality. The interviewer had even made references to artworks he had previously seen in Soyinka's house at Abeokuta and what they meant. Soyinka had written about sculpture and particularly his collection of them in his memoir,

*You Must Set Forth at Dawn.* When the interviewer wanted to know whether the collection had served as inspiration? Soyinka who had heard such gossip from Nigerian visitors, burst into prolonged laughter and said: "they have always been for aesthetics."

Humanism is important to him and he does not see morality in strict religious binaries in terms of Christians and Muslims, atheists, traditionalists, homosexuals and bi-sexuals or madmen and specialists. He seems to believe that whatever people may be they can all enjoy his friendship so long as they do not impose their beliefs on non-believers by force or through violent coercion. It was for instance out of anger and what he considered fundamental disrespect that he wrote *The Seven Signposts,* an unorthodox moral commandments based on Yoruba spirituality whose essence is not different from other religious teachings. He disagreed with the accusation that traditional Yoruba religion lacks Liturgical and Eucharistic elements and was therefore not a major force.

Soyinka used to be an Anglican and there are photos of him from his youth being groomed to be a chorister. He departed from that religious upbringing in adulthood and composed many musical arrangements, most popular among them; *Unlimited Liability Company* in which he professed patriotism with the proclamation "I love My Country." It did not debar the former Archbishop of Canterbury and a fellow poet, Rowan

Williams from encouraging him to come to Oxford because as he put it: "Soyinka is a massive cultural presence and it would be wonderful if Oxford could provide him with a platform to speak in this way." The Archbishop also agreed to share an evening platform of poetry reading with him at the University of Oxford.

What do we derive from the distinguished Irish poet, Gerard Smyth's quote that "Wole Soyinka is a poet of witness in his homeland whose moral, ethical and questioning mindset has guided his poetry and other writings?" This may well be construed as restricting Soyinka's influence to Nigeria and Africa but his legacy could be extended to the universal as Ato Quayson puts it: "A son of Africa he maybe, but he is both by choice and inclination a gift to the world."

The Nobel Prize in 1986 was not the ultimate in Soyinka's career. His productivity level after that has been unparalleled both in the history of the Nobel Institution and what should inspire any writer to continue writing after the prize. Many maybe familiar and could even think of him as the Yoruba youngster who used the cultural base of his people to create international literature.

Some of his essays have been the first to alert us to human rights abuses (lest we forget) and he was the first global writer who in 2005 alerted us to the Janjaweed militia who backed by the Sudanese government raped women, killed and forced over 2 million people into refugee status in South Sudan before it became independent. Other essays of rebuttals are directed towards people he considers irritants – "of market gossips" and of "peculiar tragedies of trained historians." One conversation even ventures into his mortality to which he asserted; "should be buried in a cactus patch in the grounds of my house" at Abeokuta, his ancestral home.

Soyinka's muse for children's literature has returned with all his white hair including the publication in 2011 of *Alapata Apata – A Play for Yorubafonia, Class for Xenophiles* which is also a universal play for all children in which the correct use of language and values, be they Yoruba, Igbo, Shona or English, must be studied and used well. It is a play of repudiation of the tonal imitation of European accents as a form of polished manners. *Travel Club* and *Boy Soldier* with the latter performed at the British National Youth Theatre.

He has through the activities of The Lumina Foundation in Lagos not only met and dined every year since 2000 with a variety of writers and audiences, but spends time to read to children at his house at Abeokuta. He takes an interest in their celebrations and literary upbringing. He has placed a self-prohibition on photography with adults but welcoming to children as he travels around the world and addresses their interests and celebrates them. His favourite musical is the Lagos-based youth band *Foot-prints of David* who often perform even if they do not perform with the musical precision of *The Lion King* but display the same energy levels and enthusiasm.

Back to nostalgia in the 1960s in Accra where he would gather children at the Ghana Drama Studio founded by his dramatist friend and colleague, Efua Sutherland and read to them, dance with them and direct plays.

When he arrived at the Ghana International School in Accra almost 50 years later, he was completely moved to hear pupils of this elite school comprising students from a variety of races and backgrounds across the world sing the school's anthem in unison. The lyrics are all that life means to Soyinka. It had been written 50 years ago by one of the pupils, Sally Fisher, most likely a European Jew in youthful innocence or in prophetic anticipation of the 21st Century global misunderstanding and violence:

I

**Ghana International School Anthem:**
From all the countries of the earth,
We come in turn to you.
Of different races, different creeds and
Different aspects too.
We learn together day by day,
In time our ways will part.

But with each one of us we'll take
Understanding of each other.

II

May we go out from this our school
In the glory of our youth.
And be prepared to live our lives
With courage, honour and truth.
And as the days pass one by one
May we be made to see
The greatest gift in life can be
Understanding of each other.

III

Of all the lessons we have learned
The greatest one must be,
That all the people of the earth,
Should live in harmony.
No need for war, no need for strife,
For we can surely see
The way towards a peaceful life
Is understanding of each other.

IV

If Soyinka had been elected the Oxford Professor of Poetry in 2015, it would have enhanced Oxford's international reputation. As the runner-up, feathers were ruffled and that engendered calls for a reflection of a marvellous career especially in the contemporary context. Unfortunately, two Nobel Laureates and world-renowned poets – the other being Derek Walcott from St. Lucia have both lost their bid for the Oxford Poetry Professorship twice in a row. Walcott had to resign from the contest due to the negative media publicity and the controversy that derailed his bid and Soyinka had to solider on in spite of it. But as he admits, he was "haunted by the nightmare of a Walcott scenario" not because of a lack of bravery but from a pattern of thinking and voting that is not in tune with universal values.

Historical models in Britain have inspired Anglophone African writing before Soyinka's generation though the raw materials in the cultural matrix had always existed in African societies. Having mastered the art and technique of dissecting the English language for their own purposes, the metropolitan masters may well feel a sense of unease about inclusiveness in what they may regard as the prestigious club of their great Western literary tradition.

It is most likely that if there is going to be one African writer among the distinguished ones both of his generation and beyond who will be read 50 years hence, it will be Wole Soyinka who in one breath could be compared in poetic terms to the German poet and playwright Bertolt Brecht and in another to the Chilean poet, diplomat and politician, Pablo Neruda and the Palestinian poet and author Mahmoud Darwish.

# CHAPTER FOUR

## On the Island of Poetry

### Literary Awards and the Canonization of African Creativity

*Tiziana Morosetti*

Of all the editions of Wole Soyinka's acclaimed poetry, the booklet *Man and Nature (Per Cleto Munari)*, first published in Italy on 13 July 2005 to celebrate Soyinka's 71st birthday, is no doubt the least known – and yet one that is illustrative of the potential of Soyinka's poetry, as well as of the character of the man himself. Published in a limited edition of one thousand copies (of which sixty are enriched with an original etching by illustrator Giuseppe Sciacca), and translated by Armando Pajalich, a pioneering scholar of African Literature and a poet himself, the volume collects some of the finest lines from *Samarkand and Other Markets I Have Known* (2002), which appear here both in English and Italian accompanied by a reproduction of autograph manuscripts of the fragments. *Man and Nature* is, in the words of Cleto

Munari, the Italian designer and design impresario to whom the booklet is dedicated, "a work whose roundness of thought turns the fragment, the isolated maxim, into […] a source of strength" (8); a "sort of finished poem" that, as we shall see, is as independent and as different as can be from Soyinka's previous collection.

Soyinka's collaboration with Munari goes back to another, perhaps more famous venture, Munari's "Five Pens" project – a set of fountain pens inspired by, alongside Soyinka, Nobel Laureates Naguib Mahfouz, Toni Morrison, José Saramago, and Saul Bellow, to contribute to which Munari invited architects Toyo Ito, Alessandro Mendini, Alvaro Siza Vieira and Oscar Tusquets Blanca. Each pen comes with a volume, *The Book of Five Pens*, which gathers the sketches for the designs, as well as some letters with the five Nobel laureates' meditations on the pen; in his, Soyinka states that he "simply cannot realise a poem except through that three-way dialogue – the mind, the pen and the obliging template of paper"[1], unlike other genres that see the involvement of a PC or a typewriter. The black-and-rhodium-plated-gold Soyinka pen can be purchased for €500.

Limited-edition volumes; luxury items; writers-designers collaboration: it may all seem very far from the "'thorn in the side' of an oppressive Nigerian polit-

1 http://www.cletomunaripens.com/immagini/press04/penna-n60-2-big.jpg

ical establishment", as Ivor Agyeman-Duah puts it in his introduction to *Essays in Honour of Wole Soyinka at 80* (2014: 1), that Soyinka has consistently been throughout his career. But, as the late Femi Johnson says, "[W]e are talking of a man of many facets" (2014: 80), and to be sure, in the life of this "[p]laywright, polemicist, mythopoieist, scholar, connoisseur of rare wine and novelist" (Ogunbiyi 2014: 85), there has been ample space for the aestheticism that characterizes a collaboration such as that with Munari. Nor has this aestheticism, the idea of an art for art's sake that may inform some of Soyinka's interests, ever prevented him from answering a fundamental "need of justice", in Nadine Gordimer's words (2014: 23); from paying personally, first with his imprisonment, then with exile, for his political views; or from grounding his writing, which stretches across virtually all genres, in a profoundly human ethos. Far more than the man of letters *only*, it is this all-encompassing, challenging personality that the unfortunate result of the 2015 election to Professor of Poetry has deprived Oxford of.

Since winning the Nobel Prize in Literature in 1986 however, Soyinka has been increasingly perceived as "dual", the picture of an "international", Western-oriented Soyinka progressively gaining ground alongside that of the locally-rooted, committed artist. While in actual reality becoming a Nobel Laureate has not affected Soyinka's creative choices, nor his capacity of involvement in the political dynamics of his country (indeed, his continent), the canonization of Soyinka through the Nobel prize has encouraged a binary reading of his writing. As Yemi Ogunbiyi has observed, "[t]here is also the additional problem of his [Soyinka's] being, in certain respects, a misunderstood man" (2014: 84), something that "can be traced to certain seemingly contradictory elements in him. Although his roots are firmly grounded in Yoruba cosmology, he is one of the most internationalist, eclectic and most travelled of our artists." While an essay such as the recent *Of Africa* (2012) very aptly shows how these elements are integrated in Soyinka's work, the decade that preceded the Nobel Prize saw more than one critic stress the existence of seemingly oppositional trends in Soyinka's career. As Michael Etherton puts it:

> Soyinka is unquestionably Africa's leading playwright, but the African audiences for his major philosophical plays are very small indeed. [...] His left-wing African critics accuse him of a reactionary sensibility and intellect; yet his political activities [...] seem to stem from a deep concern for the common man [...]. He has been consistently and passionately Pan Africanist in his public life; and yet he is often regarded elsewhere in Africa – and even in Nigeria – as narrowly Yoruba in his intellectual affinities (1982: 243).

Soyinka's drama is in particular subject to a binary interpretation, with Biodun Jeyifo juxtaposing "minor" works like *The Trials of Brother Jero*, *Jero's Metamorphosis*, *Childe Internationale*, and *The Lion and the Jewel*", which are "enormously popular", to "the major plays, the 'canonical' works, like *A Dance of the Forests*, *The Road*, *Madmen and Specialists* and *Death and the King's Horseman*", which are, on the other hand, "very infrequently performed, either at home or abroad" (1988: 92-93).

Femi Osofisan had similarly observed in 1978 that Soyinka's plays: "are structurally designed like our traditional repertory into two broad patterns of celebration. The first group would comprise those [...] whose main elements [...] are caricature and masquerade, plus an implicit or explicit moral censure. [...]. The second group of Soyinka's plays are metaphysical in content and mood [...]. Such are the plays included in Soyinka's first volume of *Collected Plays* in 1973[2]" (157)– although it is important to note that, by ascribing these diverse patterns to "our traditional repertory", Osofisan does not assume them to be incompatible.

The relevance of criticism in forging a dual construction of Soyinka is better appreciated if one considers how by the end of the 1980s, "the pattern of exchanges between writers and critics has often assumed the dimensions of a fratricidal verbal warfare occasionally degenerating to a level of adolescent name-calling: between Achebe and Nnolim over the source of *Arrow*

2 The collection includes *A Dance of the Forest*, *The Swamp Dwellers*, *The Strong Breed*, *The Road* and *The Bacchae of Euripides*.

*of God*; between Soyinka and the Ife-Ibadan School of Marxist critics [...], between Armah on the one hand and Charles Larson and his other critics on the other [...], between the Chinweizu school of *bolekaja* criticism and everybody else" (Amuta1989: 30). It is in such a climate that Soyinka was awarded the Nobel Prize.

On the one hand, there were those, like Chinweizu, for whom the Prize "by continuing European domination of African cultural expression, by rewarding extravagantly those writers whose works bear the greatest formal resemblance to those produced in the West [...] perpetuates the intellectual enslavement of Africa to its former colonial rulers" (Lindfors 1988: 481). On the other, the motives of Soyinka's writing risked being gravely misinterpreted when not openly dismissed or boycotted, by the very people who formally rejoiced in Soyinka's achievement, recognizing the Prize as honouring Nigeria and Africa as a whole. In Femi Osofisan's warning, "Soyinka is not just a prize, but a man and a citizen [...] a writer with an ardent message for his generation. But how many of us care to know [...] what really is the meaning of his work, if we insist on counting among his admirers, the rogues and predators he has so violently denounced, the inept and corrupt politicians, the mimick men in uniform, the bribe-taking and indolent bureaucrats, the shallow, pretentious professors [...]?" (1988: 187).

Both positions – regarding Soyinka as a traitor and

treating him like an empty national icon – denied Soyinka his integrity by detaching him from his cultural background, while diminishing his role in the political challenges of his country. The "contradictory critical principles underlying Nigerian aesthetic preferences", as Bernth Lindfors calls them (1988: 482), only added to this picture, as the essays that emerged after the award conveyed a composite portrait of Soyinka's work and personality, in which "Ogundipe-Leslie had Soyinka as a universalist; Okpewho saw him as an African; Irele identified him as a Nigerian; and Jeyifo […] claimed him as primordially a Yoruba" (485). At the other end of the scale, university students also showed "the same scrambled confusion," as they "were quite tolerant of Soyinka's obscurity and more than willing to salute him without understanding much of what he had written" (486). "The biggest question of all to ask about such an award" still awaited an answer: "Who in Nigeria will benefit from it? Many citizens took vicarious pleasure in Soyinka's winning of a major intellectual sweep stakes, but after sharing with him that brief glow of international recognition, will any of them be any better off than they were before?"

While it was by no means limited to Soyinka's production only, the implicit assumption that art should be socially relevant – or, rather, the fear that poetry may make nothing happen after all, to echo Auden – found fertile ground in the debate surrounding Soyinka and the Nobel Prize. To an extent, winning the Nobel Prize invested Soyinka with an even greater responsibility, as his new status implied a wider potential of intervention; at the same time, however, it was exactly this status that definitively contributed to seal the idea of an estranged, privileged public figure. The proliferation of international publications that has followed the Nobel Prize has done nothing to dispel this idea, with the register, audience and contents of collections such as the OUP-published *Open Sore of a Continent* (1996) and *The Burden of Memory, the Muse of Forgiveness* (1999) differing significantly from volumes such as the locally-published series *Interventions* (2005-2007). All however, share a robust interest and insight into things African, with Nigeria and its particular cultures often working, in Soyinka's analysis, as a touchstone for other scenarios in Africa. It is this productive kaleidoscope that has failed to be recognized by those that, for one reason or another, keep on cultivating the image of a Soyinka irremediably lost in contradiction, his writing and personality conveying, rather than complexity, unevenness and incoherence.

Once Soyinka's complexity is acknowledged, his career can also accordingly be put into perspective. Whereas the best definition for Soyinka has perhaps been given by Ngũgĩ wa Thiong'o – a "renaissance figure, dashing, defiant and daring" (2014: 22), whose seemingly oppositional poles comprise an exceptional variety of interests and activities – this definition also reflects, alas, the daunting aspect of this figure: its being, in many ways, on the verge of extinction. While the Nobel Prize has affected the *reception* of Soyinka's writing, (although arriving comparatively early in his career), it has not affected his independence of judgement and thought though other more recent awards risk nurturing writers with a much narrower, limited scope.

Of all the reactions to Soyinka's winning the Nobel Prize, the "sanest" (487), in Lindfors's view, is Chinua Achebe's presidential address at a 1986 conference of the Association of Nigerian Authors. In that address, Achebe famously declared that, Soyinka having beaten the white man at his game, African authors must now play their own – the promising nature of this auspice lying, for Lindfors, in Achebe's situating this game "a good distance from Stockholm". Thirty years later, however, it is debatable what role the prizes that have been established in the meantime, such as the Baileys Women's Prize for Fiction (previously Orange Prize for Fiction, 1996- ) and the Caine Prize for African Writing (2000- ), or the older Man Booker Prize (1969- ), may have played in this process.

An immediate impact of these awards has certainly been in narrowing the genres cultivated by authors, with the short story and above all, the novel at the forefront of the competition. Pius Adesanmi and Chris

Dunton have situated "the first real break for the third generation novel" (2005: 10) in 'Biyi Bandele's relocation to England in the early 1990s, when he began to write fiction, as well as in the later publication of three novels in particular: Helon Habila's *Waiting for an Angel*, Chris Abani's *Graceland* and Chimamanda Ngozi Adichie's *Purple Hibiscus*. However, the institutionalization of creativity through literary prizes, as well as (even more importantly) the increasing relevance of Creative Writing programmes, have produced a *specialization* of writing that is also arguably at the core of this process. It is a process that has helped many outstanding voices from Africa find recognition in recent years; and yet, on the downside, it has also partially implied a crystallization of writing from/about Africa, with productions as rich and as diversified as that of Soyinka simply becoming – should the game of African writers be played solely according to these new rules – no longer possible.

The picture is only made worse by awards such as the London-based Caine Prize for African Writing. With the Nobel Prize having been won since 1986, by only three other African writers, Naguib Mahfouz, Nadine Gordimer and J.M. Coetzee; the Man Booker Prize having gone, alongside Gordimer and Coetzee, to Ben Okri; and the Baileys Women's Prize for Fiction having been awarded only to Chimamanda Ngozi Adichie, it has been left to the Caine to best represent the African continent. However, as I have pointed out elsewhere,[3] by indirectly encouraging authors to conform to an idea of what an African writer *should be*, the Caine Prize has further contributed to narrowing the spectrum of choices for writers, nurturing replication rather than innovation in a market that, when it comes to Africa, is keen to have readers reassured in their notions. The establishment of the Nigerian-based Wole Soyinka Prize for Literature in Africa in 2005 is therefore in this context, a most welcome variation on the theme as, by supporting all genres including drama, which remains the liveliest of the arts in Africa, the Wole Soyinka Prize has reversed the trend inaugurated by other awards, thus getting a step closer to the scenario advocated by Achebe in his 1986 presidential address.

If there is a lesson that can come from Soyinka's career, this is to be found in the compelling way Soyinka has defied categorization and barriers by not only writing across genres, but also producing an opus that works at different levels.

This is the case with *Man and Nature*. As mentioned in the opening of this essay, this collection reproduces and rearranges lines from *Samarkand and Other Markets I Have Known*. While with the latter Soyinka returned "to the tight lyric verse for which he had become famous in earlier poems" (Quayson 2014: 65), the former

3 https://theconversation.com/nigerias-young-authors-are-not-always-heirs-to-their-literary-forebears-46892.

is a distillation of that work, one whose "occasional nature," in Munari's words is owed to a "friendship with those who share my love of art, design, poetry" (8). The relationship between man and nature is explored through a journey into the physical ("Wind and rain on sensuous tongue, welcome/Their rounds of impassioned cleansing," 13), the visual ("A fallen leaf, trapped briefly by the passing sun/It flashes, a mere shard of memory," 23), the political ("The xylophone of justice/ Chime much louder than the flutes of poets," 39), the metaphysical ("One road only leads to Jerusalem, only one -/That broad, pebbled spine of human oneness," 55) via the market place ("The rainbow's arc is rounded in a market place/Where scattered tribes of a busy world unite," 31) and the Yoruba religious worldview ("Man is restless seeker/What follows six, says Ifa, transcends the bounds/Of seven," 43).

Each maxim is beautiful and meaningful in its own right, lines from poems as different as "Samarkand and Other Markets I Have Known" and "Elegy for a Nation" following one another ("Let a hundred thousand/Flowers diffuse exotic incense and a million/ Stars perfume the sky," 15; "We inched towards the sun, then raced beyond/To drink the heady drought of space," 17), while others are extrapolated from context to shine independently, as with the fragments dedicated to the market place (in bold those included in *Man and Nature*, 29-33):

**The ocean meets the sea in a market place**
**And rivers down their debris on its shelves –**
Rich silt, beachcombers' treasure trove.
**The rainbow's arc is rounded in a market place**
**Where scattered tribes of a busy world unite**
Amidst the silenced blades of swords and spears
And ancient muskets, poison shafts and knobkerries.
Like guardians to that lost, miraculous edition,
Filled with lost wisdoms, lost journeys of the mind.
**The space of dreams remain inviolate,**
**Egalitarian in the market place**
Though desecration stalks in priestly garb
By surrogates, by one-eyed arbiters. (*Samarkand*, 57)

Most of the lines collected in *Man and Nature* are provided, interestingly, by politically-oriented poems such as "Some Deaths are Worlds Apart: For Kudirat," "Where the News Came to Me of the Death of a Tyrant," "Samarkand and Other Markets I Have Known: For Naguib Mahfouz" and "Elegy for a Nation: For Chinua Achebe at Seventy," The sense of a very specific political and cultural context is of course totally lost in the new collection, with the maxim "Courage is its own crown, sometimes/Of thorns, always luminous as martyrdom" (37), taken from "Some Deaths are Worlds Apart: For Kudirat," for instance, sandwiched between two fragments from "Elegy for a Nation: For Chinua Achebe:" "Ours/Are hands that always were, hands that pleat/The warp of sunbeams and the weft of dew" (35), and "The xylophones of justice…" (39).

Kudirat Abiola, wife of M.K.O. Abiola, assassinated by Sani Abacha in 1996, is in the original poem juxtaposed to Princess Diana, as "No bed of flowers bloomed for Kudirat/She was not royal, white or glamorous" (*Samarkand*, 19), but while in this poem the lines "Courage… martyrdom" are followed by an extremely specific, somewhat un-poetic list of equally remarkable women ('Her pedigree was one with Moremi/ Queen Amina, Aung Sung Kyi, with/The Maid of Orleans and all who mother/Pain as offspring, offer blood as others, milk,' *Samarkand*, 20), the fragment becomes in *Man and Nature* a universal, ungrounded hymn to a fundamental human virtue. Similarly, the other two fragments are deprived of whatsoever political meaning, while in the original poem specific references to the International Monetary Fund, the World Bank and to Levi's jeans, but also to Ogun and Sango, or, alongside Achebe, Senghor and Okigbo, come in abundance, with lines such as "Gang-raped, the continent/Turns pregnant with the word" (*Samarkand*, 71) striking a tune that is as far as possible from the idyllic wisdom conveyed in *Man and Nature.*

Had this collection had wider international resonance, it would have probably contributed, in juxtaposition to *Samarkand and Other Markets I Have Known*, to further enhance the representation of a "dual" Soyinka. As it is, however, *Man and Nature* simply highlights the potential of a writing that, encompassing the low-brow and the high-brow, the local and the universal, the political and the metaphysical, stretches through geographical, chronological and cultural boundaries. Whereas Munari's "heartfelt wish is that we may all go on enjoying many more years together on the communal island we share: the island of poetry" (8), our wish is that, on this island, a complexity and a richness such as found in Soyinka's luminous career may also characterize contemporary African writing.

## CHAPTER FIVE

# Lost Poetic Opportunity

### Had Wole Soyinka Come to Oxford

The college stone, that takes its colour
from the quality of that day's sun – now gold,
now cream, now honeycomb – its carvings
blurred by centuries of rain and wind
and yet more rain, now goes
unnoticed; every back is turned towards
the walls, as here, in modest splendour,
walks the Smith.
Bull voiced, each shoulder blade an anvil,
hammer firmly in his hand, and in his head
and heart a flame,
                                        he brings fresh iron
to this place of stone, and fire to its
banked up embers. How his eight decades
rejuvenate the ancient spires!

and every hammer blow will shake
even these deep foundations.

**Peter J. King**

## The Oxford Gig

I have never seen an Ox
let alone an ox coupled with a Ford
Oh Lord, I do not sing this with an affront
"What can't the rich afford
once they are in accord."
The Wire had it that Oxford wanted Kongi
And Kongi too wanted the Oxford gig
not so that he can boast
but to rub the nose of those who
bloodied the nose of his pal in the past.
Shall we send our thanks to Lord Bragg
Whose spanner in the works led to a sag
In that bag of votes
The elections came and went in peace
With votes cast for and against
Armitage of the nation of Tea drinking
Won more votes to pull an Ox across
the Oxford screen of words and thoughts
He will write and read his words
As a broadcaster who earned his voice

With "penniless poetry pilgrimage"
Now I can watch out for his plumage
  on the Oxford skies
and train my ears to pick up more lines
  to add to sack.

**Kole Odutola**

**Soyinka the Bold**
(to the rhythm of "Young Lochinvar")

Have you not heard of Soyinka the Bold?
In all the great houses his story is told
His body is flesh
but his mind it is gold
Oh Soyinka, Soyinka the Bold.

Soyinka the Bold and Soyinka the Brave
In Oxford his wisdom us poets did crave
Yet his victory was snatched
by a dastardly knave!
Oh Soyinka, Soyinka the Brave.

For our dearest Wole we can but thole
As a young lad from Yorkshire takes over his role
For he don't look the part
And he lacketh the soul
Of our hero of poetry, Wole.

Oh yes! Down the Cherwell we have been sold
By a Braggardly press which in muck has been rolled
And we can but mourn
Our losses untold
Of lovely Soyinka, Soyinka the Bold.
Of our lovely Soyinka the Bold.

**Jenny Lewis**

## Rage Against Age

Is there a rage against age?
The young of today will add some years
The old you scorn have no need of tears
My fear is that more things are lost
when we keep the ones with grey away
Let them come our way
Let them weigh in with their say
The young poets of today need the layers
to keep them warm when the prints are cold
The princes of critic – kingdom visited the old
they know how to call their bluff

As to the narrow tunnels
turn your necks and change channels
The world is more than a single station
The more the nations, the sweeter your position

and reflection.
I cannot help, I cannot help
when you combine fear of age
with a celebration of ideas in a cage!
Years in a cave are gone,
days of guns to win more lands
now in the pit of history
Has the empire not expired?

**Kole Odutola**

**The Repetition**

(To be sung to the tune of Leon Rosselson's "World turned upside down")

Oxford 2015, and the year was almost done –
But old battles raged; there was a grand prize to be won.
A strong Yorkshire poet, of high renown and fame
Would fend off the foreigners in Little England's name.

Six full years had passed since the fateful time
When a West Indian was dragged through muck and grime
By his British rival, keen and hungry for success,

Who campaigned against him with her chums in
the press.
Six full years had passed, but the years were not so
long
That it was forgotten she'd done a grievous wrong
To the Nobel laureate, who resigned from the
game
Once the press had damaged him and defaced his
name.

Now that Soyinka, our champion brave and true
Took up the challenge, he had much to say and do.
Smarting at injustice, smarting for his friend
He entered the lists in a fight that has no end.

"I come in peace" he said, "I hide my grudge
For the shame you laid on the man you chose to
judge.
He is the best there is. No dishonour worse –
If you have it in for me, I'll still stay the course."

"Where's your statement then, and how do you
dare
To break the rules we make which are so clear and
fair?"
"I need no statement, my deeds are eloquent –
If you seek evidence, look at how my life is spent."

# Lost Poetic Opportunity

"You are too old", they said, "too grand, too wise –
Only our countrymen are fit to win this global
prize.
You show no interest in coming here.
Stay in *your* world; you already have your share."

Formed a strong wall to keep the black man out
They gave forth a hunting cry, a loud and loyal
shout:
"Come vote with us, my lads – Enough is enough!
We value homespun worth; not all that foreign
stuff."

The votes were counted, the tournament was
through.
The winner's name, announced, cheered hearts
brave and true:
Stalwart local hearts, proud of Britannia's name –
They kept the best man out, to their eternal shame.

"I go in peace," he said. "I hide my grudge
For the shame you laid on the man you chose to
judge.
He's still the best there is. No dishonour worse –
You had it in for us, but at least I stayed the course."

**Lucy Newlyn**

# Editors and Contributors

**Lucy Newlyn** – was born in Uganda, grew up in Leeds and read English at Lady Margaret Hall, Oxford. She is now Professor of English and Literature at Oxford University and a Fellow of St Edmund Hall. She has published widely on English Romantic Literature, including four books with Oxford University Press and the Cambridge Companion to Coleridge. Together with Guy Cuthbertson, she edited *Branch Lines*: *Edward Thomas and Contemporary Poetry* for Enitharmon Press. Her first collection *Ginnel* (Carcanet) was published in 2005; and her second, *Earth's Almanac* came out in 2015, with Enitharmon.

**Ivor Agyeman-Duah** – was the inaugural curator of The John A. Kufuor Foundation Museum and Presidential Library. He is Development Policy Advisor to The Lumina Foundation that administers the Wole Soyinka Prize for Literature in Africa and was chair of the Literature Jury of the Millennium Excellence

Foundation. As a literary historian, he co-edited, *Essays in Honour of Wole Soyinka at 80 and is editor of All the Good Things Around Us: An Anthology of African Short Stories* to be published by Ayebia in 2016. *He has held Fellowships at the W. E .B. Du Bois Institute at Harvard and was a Hilary* and Trinity Visiting Fellow at Exeter College, Oxford. He holds graduate degrees from the London School of Economics (LSE) and Political Science from the School of Oriental and African Studies, London.

**Tiziana Morosetti** – teaches at the African Studies Centre at the University of Oxford. She studied in Rome and Bologna before moving to Oxford on a Marie Curie Research Fellowship with a project on the representation of the "exotic" body in nineteenth-century British drama. Her publications have appeared in *Research in African Literatures*, *West Africa Review*, *West African Theatre and Performing Arts Journal* and the Oxford Dictionary of African Biography. She is Deputy-Director of the Journal *Quaderni del '900*, for which she edited numbers IV (*Postcolonial Literature in Italian*, 2005) and VII (*Italy in Anglophone Literatures*, 2008). She is also the author of the first guide in Italian to Nigerian theatre. Since 2014 she has been membership secretary of the African Theatre Association (AfTA).

**Carmen Bugan** – is the author of the internationally acclaimed memoir *Burying the Typewriter: Childhood Under the Eye of the Secret Police*, the collections of poems *Crossing the Carpathians* and *The House of Straw*, and the monograph *Seamus Heaney and East European Poetry in Translation: Poetics of Exile*. She also presented the BBC documentary *The Man Who Went Looking for Freedom* about visiting her father's prisons in Romania.

**Peter J. King** – Lecturer in Philosophy at Pembroke College and St. Edmund Hall, Oxford, King's poetry, including co-translation from Modern Greek and German has been published in journals such as *Tears in the Fence*, *Dream Catcher* and *New Walk*. He has recently published a collection, *Adding Colours to the Chameleon*, with Wisdom's Bottom Press.

**Kole Odutola** Nigerian poet, University Lecturer in Languages and Botany in the United States, he is author of *The Poet Fled, The Poet Bled* and has received many awards for his poetry in Nigeria, Europe and the United States.

**Jenny Lewis** – Teaches creative writing (poetry) at Oxford University and is a poet, songwriter, playwright, screenwriter and children's author. Her works include the stage performance of *After Gilgamesh* (2011) and the poetry collection, *Taking Mesopotamia* (2014).

Acknowledgements

We would like to express our gratitude first to all the good people who supported efforts through their endorsement of Wole Soyinka's bid for the Oxford Professor of Poetry and those around the world who bothered to vote. Without their boldness and participation, which inspired this publication, there would not have been the opportunity to also discuss possible electoral reforms to the position of Oxford Professor of Poetry.

We owe a major debt of gratitude to Nana Ayebia Clarke MBE and David Clarke and their team at Ayebia Clarke Publishing Limited who are Oxfordshire-based Publishers and specialists in African and Caribbean writing for publishing this book for markets in Africa, Europe, United States and rest of the world. To Henry Louis Gates Jr. for the use of his thoughts on Soyinka from *A Life in Full* and for his endorsement). To Sarah Apronti, General Manager of Asempa Publishers in Accra who did the initial reading of the draft manuscript.

The version of Lucy Newlyn's essay reproduced here is a first draft of the one that appeared in the Times Higher Education (THE) on 9 July 2015, under the title "Selecting Oxford's professor of poetry should not be trial by media."

Carmen Bugan's "Wole Soyinka's Poetry: The Insistence on Liberty" was published by English PEN on 4th June 2015.

We would also like to acknowledge the Hall Writers' Forum, which served as the centre for the Soyinka Campaign for four months and where all the endorsements and poems featured here were first published.

We also acknowledge the Oxford Universty Gazette for text for Flysheet 4th Trinity Term.

# Works Cited

On the Island of Poetry: Literary Awards and the Canonization of African Creativity
*Tiziana Morosetti*

Adesanmi, Pius, and Chris Dunton (2005), "Nigeria's Third Generation Writing: Historiography and Preliminary Theoretical Considerations", *English in Africa*, 32 (1), New Nigerian Writing (May), pp. 7-19.

Agyeman-Duah, Ivor and Ogochukwu Promise, eds. (2014), *Essays in Honour of Wole Soyinka at 80*, Banbury, Ayebia Clarke Publishing Ltd.

Amuta, Chidi (1989), *The Theory of African Literature*, London, Zed Books.

Etherton, Michael (1982), *The Development of African Drama*, New York, Africana Publishing Company.

Gordimer, Nadine (2014), "For Art and Life", in Agyeman-Duah and Promise 2014, p. 23.

Jeyifo, Biodun (1988), "Wole Soyinka's Theatre", in Ogunbiyi 1988, vol. pp. 2, 92-96.

Johnson, Femi (2014) [1987], "'I Shall Go Beyond and Rest…'", in Agyeman-Duah and Promise 2014, pp. 77-82.

Lindfors, Bernth (1988), "Beating the White Man at his

Own Game: Nigerian Reactions to the 1986 Nobel Prize in Literature", Black American Literature Forum, 22 (3), Wole Soyinka Issue, Part 1 (Autumn), pp. 475-488.

Ngũgĩ wa Thiong'o (2014), "The Conscience of Africa", in Agyeman-Duah and Promise 2014, pp. 19-22.

Ogunbiyi, Yemi (1988), *Perspectives on Nigerian Literature: 1700 to the Present*, 2 vol., Lagos, Guardian Books Ltd.

– (2014)[1987], "Let Us Think Again," in Agyeman-Duah and Promise 2014, pp. 83-88.

Osofisan, Femi (1978), "Tiger on Stage: Wole Soyinka and Nigerian Theatre", in Oyin Ogunba and Abiola Irele, eds., *Theatre in Africa*, Ibadan, Ibadan University Press, 1978, pp. 151-75.

– (1988), "Soyinka in the Forest of a Thousand Revellers," in Ogunbiyi 1988, vol. 1, pp. 186-89.

Quayson, Ato (2014), "All of the People, Some of the Time:" The Ethics of Choice in a Soyinkan Action, in Agyeman-Duah and Promise 2014, pp 65-73.

Soyinka, Wole (2002), *Samarkand and Other Markets I Have Known*, London, Methuen.

– (2005) *Man and Nature (Per Cleto Munari)*, Marco Fazzini ed., Lugo, Edizioni del Bradipo.

## Text for Flysheet: Oxford University Gazette 4th Week Trinity Term

We ask you to vote for **Wole Soyinka** (Nobel Laureate, 1986) in the coming election for Professor of Poetry at Oxford.

We believe that Soyinka would be an outstanding successor to Geoffrey Hill – someone capable of inspiring us with his published work, his vision of what literature is, and his way of talking about poetry. It would be especially invigorating to have someone in this post who is able to bring an African and global perspective to the study and understanding of poetry in Oxford. We would also appreciate very deeply Soyinka's ability to talk about poetry as a practising poet, dramatist, novelist, memoirist, and human rights activist.

Professor Soyinka has taught at Cornell, Emory, and the University of Lagos. He has been awarded Honorary Doctorates by the Universities of Leeds, Harvard and Princeton. He has received the Benson Medal from the Royal Society of Literature, the Anisfield-Wolf Book Award for Lifetime Achievement, and the 2014 International Humanist Award. On becoming the first African writer to be awarded the Nobel Prize for Literature, the Swedish Academy praised Soyinka for his ability "to synthesise a very rich heritage from his own country with literary legacies and traditions of

European culture", for his "genuine and impressive creativity as an artist, a master of language", and for his commitment to exploring "problems of general and deep significance for man, modern or ancient".

In addition to his literary credentials, Wole Soyinka has a track record in campaigning for human rights that puts him in a unique category. He was a powerful voice in the struggle for Nigeria's independence from colonial rule, and has been a thorn in the side of a series of Nigerian dictators. Despite considerable risk to his personal safety, he has consistently spoken out against corruption and the abuse of power. Under the government of General Gowon he suffered two years solitary confinement. A later military ruler, General Sani Abacha, charged him with treason in 1997 and sentenced him to death in absentia. Soyinka's passion for justice has never dimmed. He recently joined his fellow Nigerians in street protests against the removal of fuel subsidies; and he has played a prominent role in the "bring back our girls" campaign for the government to rescue the 219 school children abducted from Chibok by Boko Haram insurgents.

Given his lifetime of campaigning, it is a great testament to the quality and impact of Soyinka's writings that he is known first and foremost as an author, not a political activist. Amongst Soyinka's best known works, which are read world-wide, are his volumes of poetry: *Idanre and Other Poems*, *Poems from Prison*,

*A Shuttle in the Crypt*, and *Mandela's Earth*. His most famous plays include *The Lion and the Jewel* and *Death and The King's Horseman*. He has written two novels, *The Interpreter* and *Season of Anomy*, as well as five highly acclaimed autobiographical works: *Aké*, *Isara*, *Ibadan*, *You Must Set off at Dawn*, and *The Man Died: Prison Notes*. Wole Soyinka's writings provide a vital and compelling insight into personal, social and political relations with global relevance. His work taps into a host of different mythic, poetic, and dramatic traditions – African and European – and dynamically re-routes the connections between them. As an essayist, the depth, range, and erudition of his thinking about culture have emerged in volumes such as *Art, Dialogue, and Outrage: Essays on Literature and Culture*, *The Burden of Memory*, and *The Muse of Forgiveness*. In 2004, he was invited to deliver the BBC Reith Lectures, which he called *A Climate of Fear*.

Wole Soyinka's world stature is incontestable. As the first African elected to this post, his appointment would be an immense historical milestone for Oxford University. He is an inspirational speaker, whose fascinating lectures would attract large, attentive, international audiences. Please join us in voting for him as our next Professor of Poetry.

Jonathan Bate, Provost of Worcester

William Beinart, Rhodes Professor of Race Relations, St Antony's

Elleke Boehmer, Professor of World Literature in English, Wolfson

Charles Conn, Warden of Rhodes House, Balliol

Sos Eltis, Fellow in English, Brasenose

Keith Gull, Principal of St Edmund Hall

Ken Macdonald, Warden of Wadham

Jonathan Michie, Director of the Department for Continuing Education, President of Kellogg

Ankhi Mukherjee, Fellow in English, Wadham

Lucy Newlyn, Fellow in English, St Edmund Hall

Stephen Tuck, Director of The Oxford Research Centre for the Humanities, Pembroke

Wes Williams, Fellow in French, St Edmund Hall